The Open Source Conundrum

Christer Foghagen

Introduction

This paper is a reflection on the logic process of development projects and especially software development. During the 1980's and 1990's the old development logic was challenged by **open participation** *over the internet. Software companies went from being producers of software as their primary commodity to service producers with a focus on long term service relations.*

Closed source vendors increasingly focused on collecting 'big data' by offering software services free of charge as long as the user accept routine surveillance and tracking. It is important to increase the public awareness of 'concealed' functionalities in programs and applications and how these applications collect data. Recent years there has been a growing concern about the magnitude of data collection by applications which, among other things, lead to the EU data protection law (GDPR). Since the awareness of injust routine surveillance and data collection seems to be increasingly concerning for user, transparent processes might be beneficial for software vendors in the future.

Förlag: BoD – Books on Demand, Stockholm, Sverige
Tryck: BoD – Books on Demand, Norderstedt, Tyskland
ISBN: 9789180076067

Table of Contents

- 1. How to make money while giving technology away for free?
    - 1.1. Symbolic start
    - 1.2. A new development logic
    - 1.3. Raymond and The Bazar model
    - 1.4. How to make money
- 2. Conclusions
- Appendix
- Your notes and comments

1 How to make money while giving technology away for free?

Nineteen Eighty-Four (1984[1, 2]), an influencial novel written by the author George Orwell in the late 1940's. The events of the book take place in a dystopian future state called Oceania. The main character (or protagonist), Winston, appears to be a obidient and diligent citizen but he is secretly nurturing dreams of rebellion due to his hatred for Big Brother[3] and the ruling Party. The ever gazing eyes of Big Brother and the relentless hunt for apostates had refined the methods of gouvernment surveillance in Oceania. Winston and his fellow citizens was fully aware that Big Brother were watching them through the telescreens. He also knew that every move and every thought could be interpreted as an hostile act and therefore punished.

This is fiction of course. But in many ways, the fiction has become unpleasantly omnipresent today, 2021[4]. Big Brother comes in many shapes and forms. It is however important to emphasize, that there are at least as many differences as there are commonalities between the Orwellian 1984 and the world of 2021. Society as described in the novel, 1984, was a dystopian dictatorship while the real world of 2021, especially due to the past 70 years, have become increasingly democratic (i.e. since George Orwell wrote the novel 'Nineteen Eighty-Four'). Technologic advancements over the past thirty years however, have helped facilitate mass-surveillance and tracking at a scale never seen before (Yes, I dare to say that…). The dominant actors in collecting and processing 'big data'[5] are mega corporations and research institutions alongside governments and the primary aim is intelligence and business rather than to suppress people. The *Orwellian Big Brother role* had suppressive purposes. Of course, the technology has improved the ability for governments, and private companies, to collect data, process and analyse that data to detect security threats to countries and citizens. Authorities benefit from collaborating with private corporations. Although, there is a risk that data is collected on routine rather than on suspicion. It is also an apparent risk that peoples trust can be violated by companies or individuals with access to collected data. Big Brother of today is kind of a *shape shifter*, big companies and malicious individuals (*Black Hat crackers*) on one hand and authorities on the other. Therefore, Big Brother of today is more complex and much harder to identify than in the novel 1984. 'Big Data' is the new Klondike[6] or El Dorado[7] and mega-corporations collect it for money rather than to reign politically over land and people.

Commonalities between the dystopic 1984 and today are to be found in the way technology facilitate data collection, surveillance and tracking. It may also affect peoples behavior, social interaction and democratic processes[8]. That does not necessarily mean that the outcomes are negative 'by default'. On the contrary, many aspects of those technologies are positive. There are numerous proofs of that, like the Arab spring[9], Wikileaks[10], free press movements[11], revelations by whistle blowers[12] like Edward Snowden[13] and others, as well as all the social, political, financial and cultural benefits brought to us by this technology.

It is however crucial, to avoid routine surveillance and potential injustices, to increase the public awareness of 'concealed' functionalities in programs and applications and to promote user control on data-collection. The EU is currently trying to increase the protection of personal data through regulations (i.e. GDPR[14]). But just as important is for users to be aware and informed. Another way is to promote free and open source software which makes it possible for users to study the source code and understand what the program do (i.e. if there are any malicious functionalities or spyware).

1.1 Symbolic start

The year 1984 was the year when Richard
Stallman[15],[16],[17], a former PhD-student in
physics and co-worker at the *MIT* [18] *Artificial
Intelligence Lab* [19], quit his job to set out on a
quest to write a free Unix-like operating
system. The idea and project started 1983 but
sofware development started 1984 with the
founding of the Free Software Foundation
(FSF[20]). He called the project GNU[21], as in
GNU is Not Unix and the idea was double
folded. One aim was to make technology
accessible by giving away the source code and
another aim was to protect peoples rights. By
the year 1991, the GNU system was almost
completed but the most central piece of an OS,
the kernel[22],[23], was missing. The GNU-
projects had their own kernel, the 'Hurd' (or
GNU Hurd), but their kernel was not
complete. Instead Linus Thorvalds[24], a
computer science student from the University
of Helsinki[25], Finland, released his kernel,

Linux. Together the two, GNU and Linux, completed the GNU/Linux operating system.

1.2 A new development logic

Software development in the 1970's and 1980's was primarily a closed process with limited source code access for outsiders. Computer science emerged at a time and in a context of which the existing and available methods for problem solving was insufficient. The need for high speed calculations of the North American sensus (1890) gave birth to the 'Punched Charts', The German 'Enigma machine' during the World War II were solved by applying science (mainly physics), math and engineering which fostered more applications to solve problems of military nature. A growing demand for such applications especially during the post-war and cold war context stimulated the development of computers and computer science[26]. There was a strong legacy from military needs and engineering methods which affected the early field of computer science. Software companies developed their code in secrecy, aiming to sell licences of the finished proprietary product to endusers. Thanks to a military project in the 1960's, called *Arpanet* [27], the foundation were laid to transform the organizational aspects of software development. During the 1980's and 1990's the old development logic was challenged by **open participation** over the internet. Instead of leaving a small team of engineers to develop software, a community of programmers and designers could do it together over the internet. That way it became an open process of 'peer review' making the software gradually form and improve as potential bugs were detected at an early stage. 'More Eyeballs on the code' increase the chance to detect, intentional or unintentional, errors.

1.3 Raymond and The Bazar model

The software engineer, programmer, hacker and open source developer Eric S. Raymond[28], had an important role to play in the formation of community based open source software. He wrote a paper in the mid 1990's called *The Cathedral and the Bazar: Musings on Linux and Open Source by an Accidental Revolutionary* [29], in which he argues that the Bazar model, used in the Linux kernel project, is the most beneficial in terms of production, security and to improve the code quality among other things. This paper got an emblematic status and became almost synonymous with the open source and free software movements. The implications of the paper are numerous but one concrete example is that it had an immediate effect on the decision by *Netscape* [30] to give away their source code.

1.4 How to make money

Many software companies have specialized in developing free and open source software. That does not automatically mean that they give everything away for free. The source code is free for everyone to see and often to share (depending on the licencing). Many vendors of for example GNU/Linux distributions (such as

RedHat, Ubuntu and Suse Linux) provide desktop versions free of charge (Fedora, Ubuntu, and Open Suse) while they charge for customer-support and cloud services and other things on the enterprise level and for server services.

2 Conclusions

Four major implications:

1. The Bazar model can serve as an improved way to organize development projects
2. More eyeballs on the code is beneficial to ensure quality and security
3. New business logics - from software products to service providers. Today we use software as a service in, for example, cloud computing. Software, in that case, is a service provided 'free of charge' as a means to collect data.
4. Even though it takes time, users are increasingly concerned about routine collection of data[31, 32] - transparancy builds trust - hopefully, the future

might just require more of openness and transparancy

The Bazar model of software development did not only affect the way software projects were organized it also changed the business logic of software production. **Software companies went from being producers of software as their primary commodity to service producers with a focus on long term service relations.** The focus is produce and maintain good and fruitful customer relations through the provision of reliable and high quality software services. Software, customer-support and additional services like cloud computing and data-storage are strong incentives for developing lojal customers and users. This means that it is possible to make money by giving your technology away. The technology is merely the means to attract customers, the extra services provided can often be the dealbreaker! **Since the**

awareness of injust routine surveillance and data collection seems to be increasingly concerning for user transparent processes might be beneficial in the future. This is what the Free- and Open Source movements is all about. If transparency is one of the *unique selling points* of the future, closed source and proprietary software have a very rough road ahead.

Christer Foghagen, 2021

Footnotes:

1

http://www.bbc.com/culture/story/20180507-why-orwells-1984-could-be-about-now

2

https://en.wikipedia.org/wiki/Nineteen_Eighty-Four

3

https://en.wikipedia.org/wiki/
Big_Brother_(NineteenEighty-Four)

4

http://www.bbc.com/culture/story/20180507-
why-orwells-1984-could-be-about-now

5

https://en.wikipedia.org/wiki/Big_data

6

https://en.wikipedia.org/wiki/
Klondike_Gold_Rush

7

https://en.wikipedia.org/wiki/El_Dorado

8

https://www.economist.com/technology-
quarterly/2018/06/02/increased-amounts-of-
data-and-surveillance-are-transforming-
justice-systems

9

https://en.wikipedia.org/wiki/Arab_Spring

10

https://en.wikipedia.org/wiki/WikiLeaks

11

https://en.wikipedia.org/wiki/
Freedom_of_the_Press_Foundation

12

https://en.wikipedia.org/wiki/Whistleblower

13

https://en.wikipedia.org/wiki/
Edward_Snowden

14

https://en.wikipedia.org/wiki/
General_Data_Protection_Regulation

15

https://www.britannica.com/biography/
Richard-Matthew-Stallman

16

https://en.wikipedia.org/wiki/
Richard_Stallman

17

https://www.youtube.com/watch?
v=Gnw_K5DPkbc

18

https://en.wikipedia.org/wiki/
Massachusetts_Institute_of_Technology

19

https://en.wikipedia.org/wiki/
MIT_Computer_Science_and_Artificial_Intell
igence_Laboratory

20

https://www.fsf.org/

21

https://en.wikipedia.org/wiki/GNU

22

https://www.webopedia.com/TERM/K/
kernel.html

23

https://techterms.com/definition/kernel

24

https://en.wikipedia.org/wiki/Linus_Torvalds

25

https://en.wikipedia.org/wiki/
University_of_Helsinki

26

https://www.livescience.com/20718-computer-
history.html

27

https://en.wikipedia.org/wiki/ARPANET

28

https://en.wikipedia.org/wiki/
Eric_S._Raymond

29

http://www.catb.org/~esr/writings/cathedral-
bazaar/cathedral-bazaar/index.html

30

https://en.wikipedia.org/wiki/Netscape

31

https://www.economist.com/technology-quarterly/2018/06/02/increased-amounts-of-data-and-surveillance-are-transforming-justice-systems

32

http://www.pewinternet.org/2015/05/20/americans-attitudes-about-privacy-security-and-surveillance/

Author: Christer Foghagen

First draft created: 2019-02-21 tor 15:51

Revision: 2021-01-13

Emacs 25.2.2 (Org mode 8.2.10)

Validate

Appendix

This paper was initially written in Emacs org-mode and exported to html. Since open source is the main theme I decided, as an odd and somewhat quirky thing, to include the 'paper source code' in this appendix.

The Source Code

```
<?xml version="1.0" encoding="utf-8"?>
<!DOCTYPE html PUBLIC "-//W3C//DTD XHTML 1.0 Strict//EN"
"http://www.w3.org/TR/xhtml1/DTD/xhtml1-strict.dtd">
<html xmlns="http://www.w3.org/1999/xhtml" lang="en"
xml:lang="en">
<head>
<title>The Open Source Conundrum</title>
<!-- 2019-02-21 tor 15:51 -->
<meta  http-equiv="Content-Type" content="text/html;charset=utf-8"
/>
<meta  name="generator" content="Org-mode" />
<meta  name="author" content="Christer Foghagen" />
<style type="text/css">
<!--/*--><![CDATA[/*><!--*/
 .title  { text-align: center; }
 .todo   { font-family: monospace; color: red; }
 .done   { color: green; }
 .tag    { background-color: #eee; font-family: monospace;
         padding: 2px; font-size: 80%; font-weight: normal; }
 .timestamp { color: #bebebe; }
 .timestamp-kwd { color: #5f9ea0; }
 .right { margin-left: auto; margin-right: 0px;  text-align: right; }
 .left  { margin-left: 0px;  margin-right: auto; text-align: left; }
 .center { margin-left: auto; margin-right: auto; text-align: center; }
 .underline { text-decoration: underline; }
 #postamble p, #preamble p { font-size: 90%; margin: .2em; }
 p.verse { margin-left: 3%; }
```

```css
pre {
  border: 1px solid #ccc;
  box-shadow: 3px 3px 3px #eee;
  padding: 8pt;
  font-family: monospace;
  overflow: auto;
  margin: 1.2em;
}
pre.src {
  position: relative;
  overflow: visible;
  padding-top: 1.2em;
}
pre.src:before {
  display: none;
  position: absolute;
  background-color: white;
  top: -10px;
  right: 10px;
  padding: 3px;
  border: 1px solid black;
}
pre.src:hover:before { display: inline;}
pre.src-sh:before    { content: 'sh'; }
pre.src-bash:before  { content: 'sh'; }
pre.src-emacs-lisp:before { content: 'Emacs Lisp'; }
pre.src-R:before     { content: 'R'; }
pre.src-perl:before  { content: 'Perl'; }
pre.src-java:before  { content: 'Java'; }
pre.src-sql:before   { content: 'SQL'; }

table { border-collapse:collapse; }
caption.t-above { caption-side: top; }
caption.t-bottom { caption-side: bottom; }
td, th { vertical-align:top;  }
th.right  { text-align: center;  }
th.left   { text-align: center;  }
th.center { text-align: center; }
td.right  { text-align: right;  }
td.left   { text-align: left;  }
td.center { text-align: center; }
dt { font-weight: bold; }
.footpara:nth-child(2) { display: inline; }
```

.footpara { display: block; }
.footdef { margin-bottom: 1em; }
.figure { padding: 1em; }
.figure p { text-align: center; }
.inlinetask {
  padding: 10px;
  border: 2px solid gray;
  margin: 10px;
  background: #ffffcc;
}
#org-div-home-and-up
 { text-align: right; font-size: 70%; white-space: nowrap; }
textarea { overflow-x: auto; }
.linenr { font-size: smaller }
.code-highlighted { background-color: #ffff00; }
.org-info-js_info-navigation { border-style: none; }
#org-info-js_console-label
  { font-size: 10px; font-weight: bold; white-space: nowrap; }
.org-info-js_search-highlight
  { background-color: #ffff00; color: #000000; font-weight: bold; }
/*]]>*/-->
</style>
<script type="text/javascript">
/*

@licstart The following is the entire license notice for the
JavaScript code in this tag.

Copyright (C) 2012-2013 Free Software Foundation, Inc.

The JavaScript code in this tag is free software: you can
redistribute it and/or modify it under the terms of the GNU
General Public License (GNU GPL) as published by the Free
Software
Foundation, either version 3 of the License, or (at your option)
any later version. The code is distributed WITHOUT ANY
WARRANTY;
without even the implied warranty of MERCHANTABILITY or
FITNESS
FOR A PARTICULAR PURPOSE. See the GNU GPL for more
details.

As additional permission under GNU GPL version 3 section 7, you
may distribute non-source (e.g., minimized or compacted) forms of

that code without the copy of the GNU GPL normally required by section 4, provided you include this license notice and a URL through which recipients can access the Corresponding Source.


```
@licend  The above is the entire license notice
for the JavaScript code in this tag.
*/
<!--/*--><![CDATA[/*><!--*/
function CodeHighlightOn(elem, id)
{
  var target = document.getElementById(id);
  if(null != target) {
    elem.cacheClassElem = elem.className;
    elem.cacheClassTarget = target.className;
    target.className = "code-highlighted";
    elem.className   = "code-highlighted";
  }
}
function CodeHighlightOff(elem, id)
{
  var target = document.getElementById(id);
  if(elem.cacheClassElem)
    elem.className = elem.cacheClassElem;
  if(elem.cacheClassTarget)
    target.className = elem.cacheClassTarget;
}
/*]]>*///-->
</script>
</head>
<body>
<div id="content">
<h1 class="title">The Open Source Conundrum</h1>
<div id="table-of-contents">
<h2>Table of Contents</h2>
<div id="text-table-of-contents">
<ul>
<li><a href="#sec-1">1. How to make money while giving
technology away for free?</a>
<ul>
<li><a href="#sec-1-1">1.1. Symbolic start</a></li>
<li><a href="#sec-1-2">1.2. A new development logic</a></li>
```

<li><a href="#sec-1-3">1.3. Raymond and The Bazar model</a></li>
<li><a href="#sec-1-4">1.4. How to make money</a></li>
</ul>
</li>
<li><a href="#sec-2">2. Conclusions</a></li>
</ul>
</div>
</div>
<div id="outline-container-sec-1" class="outline-2">
<h2 id="sec-1"><span class="section-number-2">1</span> How to make money while giving technology away for free?</h2>
<div class="outline-text-2" id="text-1">
<p>
<i><b>Nineteen Eighty-Four (1984^{<a id="fnr.1" name="fnr.1" class="footref" href="#fn.1">1</a>}[,]^{<a id="fnr.2" name="fnr.2" class="footref" href="#fn.2">2</a>}), an influencial novel written by the author George Orwell in the late 1940's. The events of the book take place in a dystopian future state called Oceania. The main character (or protagonist), Winston, appears to be a obidient and diligent citizen but he is secretly nurturing dreams of rebellion due to his hate for Big Brother^{<a id="fnr.3" name="fnr.3" class="footref" href="#fn.3">3</a>} and the ruling Party. The ever gazing eyes of Big Brother and the relentless hunt for apostates had refined the methods of gouvernment surveillance in Oceania. Winston and his fellow citizens was fully aware that Big Brother were watching them through the telescreens. He also knew that every move and every thought could be interpreted as an hostile act and therefore punished.</b></i>
</p>

<p>
This is fiction of course. But in many ways, the fiction has become unpleasently omnipresent today, 2019^{<a id="fnr.4" name="fnr.4" class="footref" href="#fn.4">4</a>}. Big Brother comes in many shapes and forms. It is however important to emphasize, that there are at least as many differences as there are commonalities between the Orwellian 1984 and the world of 2019. Society as described in the novel, 1984, was a dystopian dictatorship while the real world of 2019, especially due to the past 70 years, have become increasingly democratic (i.e. since George Orwell wrote the novel 'Nineteen Eighty-Four').

Technologic advancements over the past thirty years however, have helped facilitate mass-surveillance and tracking at a scale never seen before (Yes, I dare to say that…). The dominant actors in collecting and processing 'big data'^{<a id="fnr.5" name="fnr.5" class="footref" href="#fn.5">5</a>} are mega corporations and research institutions alongside governments and the primary aim is intelligence and business rather than to suppress people. The Orwellian Big Brother role had suppressive purposes. Of course, the technology has improved the ability for governments, and private companies, to collect data, process and analyse that data to detect security threats to countries and citizens. Authorities benefit from collaborating with private corporations. Although, there is a risk that data is collected on routine rather than on suspicion. It is also an apparent risk that peoples trust can be violated by companies or individuals with access to collected data. Big Brother of today is kind of a shape shifter, big companies and malicious individuals (Black Hat crackers) on one hand and authorities on the other. Therefore, Big Brother of today is more complex and much harder to identify than in the novel 1984. Big Data is the new Klondike^{<a id="fnr.6" name="fnr.6" class="footref" href="#fn.6">6</a>} or El Dorado^{<a id="fnr.7" name="fnr.7" class="footref" href="#fn.7">7</a>} and mega-corporations collect it for money rather than to reign politically over land and people.
</p>

<p>
Commonalities between the dystopic 1984 and today are to be found in the way technology facilitate data collection, surveillance and tracking. It may also affect peoples behavior, social interaction and democratic processes^{<a id="fnr.8" name="fnr.8" class="footref" href="#fn.8">8</a>}. That does not necessarily mean that the outcomes are negative 'by default'. On the contrary, many aspects of those technologies are positive. There are numerous proofs of that, like the Arab spring^{<a id="fnr.9" name="fnr.9" class="footref" href="#fn.9">9</a>}, Wikileaks^{<a id="fnr.10" name="fnr.10" class="footref" href="#fn.10">10</a>}, free press movements^{<a id="fnr.11" name="fnr.11" class="footref" href="#fn.11">11</a>}, revelations by whistle blowers^{<a id="fnr.12" name="fnr.12" class="footref" href="#fn.12">12</a>} like Edward Snowden<sup><a id="fnr.13" name="fnr.13" class="footref" href="#fn.13">13</a></

sup> and others, as well as all the social, political, financial and cultural benefits brought to us by this technology.
</p>

<p>
It is however crucial, to avoid routine surveillance and potential injustices, to increase the public awareness of 'concealed' functionalities in programs and applications and to promote user control on data-collection. The EU is currently trying to increase the protection of personal data through regulations (i.e. GDPR^{<a id="fnr.14" name="fnr.14" class="footref" href="#fn.14">14</a>}). But just as important is for users to be aware and informed. Another way is to promote free and open source software which makes it possible for users to study the source code and understand what the program do (i.e. if there are any malicious functionalities or spyware).
</p>
</div>

<div id="outline-container-sec-1-1" class="outline-3">
<h3 id="sec-1-1"><span class="section-number-3">1.1</span> Symbolic start</h3>
<div class="outline-text-3" id="text-1-1">
<p>
The year 1984 is the year when Richard Stallman^{<a id="fnr.15" name="fnr.15" class="footref" href="#fn.15">15</a>} [,]^{<a id="fnr.16" name="fnr.16" class="footref" href="#fn.16">16</a>} [,]^{<a id="fnr.17" name="fnr.17" class="footref" href="#fn.17">17</a>}, a former PhD-student in physics and co-worker at the <i>MIT</i> ^{<a id="fnr.18" name="fnr.18" class="footref" href="#fn.18">18</a>} <i>Artificial Intelligence Lab</i> ^{<a id="fnr.19" name="fnr.19" class="footref" href="#fn.19">19</a>}, quit his job to set out on a quest to write a free Unix-like operating system. The idea and project started 1983 but sofware development started 1984 with the founding of the Free Software Foundation (FSF^{<a id="fnr.20" name="fnr.20" class="footref" href="#fn.20">20</a>}). He called the project GNU^{<a id="fnr.21" name="fnr.21" class="footref" href="#fn.21">21</a>}, as in <i>GNU is Not Unix</i> and the idea was double folded. One aim was to make technology accessible by giving away the source code and another aim was to protect peoples rights.

By the year 1991, the GNU system was almost completed but the most central piece of an OS, the kernel^{<a id="fnr.22" name="fnr.22" class="footref" href="#fn.22">22</a>}[,]^{<a id="fnr.23" name="fnr.23" class="footref" href="#fn.23">23</a>}, was missing. The GNU-projects had their own kernel, the 'Hurd' (or GNU Hurd), but their kernel was not complete. Instead Linus Thorvalds^{<a id="fnr.24" name="fnr.24" class="footref" href="#fn.24">24</a>}, a computer science student from the University of Helsinki^{<a id="fnr.25" name="fnr.25" class="footref" href="#fn.25">25</a>}, Finland, released his kernel, Linux. Together the two, GNU and Linux, completed the GNU/Linux operating system.
</p>
</div>
</div>

<div id="outline-container-sec-1-2" class="outline-3">
<h3 id="sec-1-2"><span class="section-number-3">1.2</span> A new development logic</h3>
<div class="outline-text-3" id="text-1-2">
<p>
Software development in the 1970's and 1980's was primarily a closed process with limited source code access for outsiders. Computer science emerged at a time and in a context of which the existing and available methods for problem solving was insufficient. The need for high speed calculations of the North American sensus (1890) gave birth to the 'Punched Charts', The German 'Enigma machine' during the World War II were solved by applying science (mainly physics), math and engineering which fostered more applications to solve problems of military nature the. A growing demand for such applications especially during the post-war and cold war context stimulated the development of computers and computer science^{<a id="fnr.26" name="fnr.26" class="footref" href="#fn.26">26</a>}. There was a strong legacy from military needs and engineering methods which affected the early field of computer science. Software companies developed their code in secrecy, aiming to sell licences of the finished proprietary product to endusers.
Thanks to a military project in the 1960's, called <i>Arpanet</i>^{<a id="fnr.27" name="fnr.27" class="footref" href="#fn.27">27</a>}, the foundation were laid to transform the organizational aspects of software development. During the 1980's and 1990's the old development logic was challenged by open

participation over the internet. Instead of leaving a small team of engineers to develop software, a community of programmers and designers could do it together over the internet. That way it became an open process of 'peer review' making the software gradually form and improve as potential bugs were detected at an early stage. 'More Eyeballs on the code' increase the chance to detect, intentional or unintentional, errors.

</p>
</div>
</div>

<div id="outline-container-sec-1-3" class="outline-3">
<h3 id="sec-1-3"><span class="section-number-3">1.3</span>
Raymond and The Bazar model</h3>
<div class="outline-text-3" id="text-1-3">
<p>

The software engineer, programmer, hacker and open source developer Eric S. Raymond^{<a id="fnr.28" name="fnr.28" class="footref" href="#fn.28">28</a>}*, had an important role to play in the formation of community based open source software. He wrote a paper in the mid 1990's called* <i>*The Cathedral and the Bazar: Musings on Linux and Open Source by an Accidental Revolutionary*</i> ^{<a id="fnr.29" name="fnr.29" class="footref" href="#fn.29">29</a>}*, in which he argues that the Bazar model, used in the Linux kernel project, is the most beneficial in terms of production, security and to improve the code quality among other things. This paper got an emblematic status and became almost synonymous with the open source and free software movements. The implications of the paper are numerous but one concrete example is that it had an immediate effect on the decision by* <i>*Netscape*</i> ^{<a id="fnr.30" name="fnr.30" class="footref" href="#fn.30">30</a>} *to give away their source code.*
</p>
</div>
</div>

<div id="outline-container-sec-1-4" class="outline-3">
<h3 id="sec-1-4"><span class="section-number-3">1.4</span>
How to make money</h3>
<div class="outline-text-3" id="text-1-4">
<p>

Many software companies have specialized in developing free and open source software. That does not automatically mean that they give everything away for free. The source code is free for everyone to see and often to share (depending on the licencing). Many vendors of for example GNU/Linux distributions (such as RedHat, Ubuntu and Suse Linux) provide desktop versions free of charge (Fedora, Ubuntu, and Open Suse) while they charge for customer-support and cloud services and other things on the enterprise level and for server services.

</p>
</div>
</div>
</div>

<div id="outline-container-sec-2" class="outline-2">
<h2 id="sec-2"><span class="section-number-2">2</span> Conclusions</h2>
<div class="outline-text-2" id="text-2">
<p>
Four major implications:
</p>
</div>

<ol class="org-ol"><li><a id="sec-2-0-0-1" name="sec-2-0-0-1"></a>*The Bazar model can serve as an improved way to organize development projects (as such, even destination development)*
</li>
<li><a id="sec-2-0-0-2" name="sec-2-0-0-2"></a>*More eyeballs on the code is beneficial to ensure quality and security*
</li>
<li><a id="sec-2-0-0-3" name="sec-2-0-0-3"></a>*New business logics - from software products to service providers. Today we use software as a service in, for example, cloud computing. Software, in that case, is a service provided 'free of charge' as a means to collect data.*
</li>
<li><a id="sec-2-0-0-4" name="sec-2-0-0-4"></a>*Even though it takes time, users are increasingly concerned about routine collection of data*^{<a id="fnr.31" name="fnr.31" class="footref" href="#fn.31">31</a>}[,]^{<a id="fnr.32" name="fnr.32" class="footref" href="#fn.32">32</a>} *- transparancy builds trust - hopefully, the future might just require more of openness and transparancy*
<div class="outline-text-5" id="text-2-0-0-4">
<p>

The Bazar model of software development did not only affect the way software projects were organized it also changed the business logic of software production. Software companies went from being producers of software as the primary commodity to service producers with a focus on long term service relations.

The focus is produce and maintain good and fruitful customer relations through the provision of reliable and high quality software services. Software, customer-support and additional services like cloud computing and data-storage are strong incentives for developing lojal customers and users.

This means that it is possible to make money by giving your technology away. The technology is merely the means to attract customers, the extra services provided can often be the dealbreaker! Since the awareness of injust routine surveillance and data collection seems to be increasingly concerning for user transparent processes might be beneficial in the future. This is what the Free- and Open Source movements is all about. If transparency is one of the <i>*unique selling points*</i> *of the future, closed source and proprietary software have a very rough road ahead.*
</p>

<p>
<b>⊚ *Copyleft:* <i>*Christer Foghagen, 2019, 2021.*</i></b>
</p>
</div>
</li></ol>
</div>
<div id="footnotes">
<h2 class="footnotes">Footnotes: </h2>
<div id="text-footnotes">

<div class="footdef">^{<a id="fn.1" name="fn.1" class="footnum" href="#fnr.1">1</a>} <p class="footpara">
<a href="http://www.bbc.com/culture/story/20180507-why-orwells-1984-could-be-about-now">http://www.bbc.com/culture/story/20180507-why-orwells-1984-could-be-about-now</a>
</p></div>

<div class="footdef">^{<a id="fn.2" name="fn.2" class="footnum" href="#fnr.2">2</a>} <p class="footpara">
<a href="https://en.wikipedia.org/wiki/Nineteen_Eighty-Four">https://en.wikipedia.org/wiki/Nineteen_Eighty-Four</a>
</p></div>

<div class="footdef"><sup><a id="fn.3" name="fn.3"
class="footnum" href="#fnr.3">3</a></sup> <p class="footpara">
<a
href="https://en.wikipedia.org/wiki/Big_Brother">https://en.wikipedi
a.org/wiki/Big_Brother</a><sub>(Nineteen_{Eighty}-
Four)</sub>
</p></div>

<div class="footdef"><sup><a id="fn.4" name="fn.4"
class="footnum" href="#fnr.4">4</a></sup> <p class="footpara">
<a href="http://www.bbc.com/culture/story/20180507-why-orwells-
1984-could-be-about-now">http://www.bbc.com/culture/story/
20180507-why-orwells-1984-could-be-about-now</a>
</p></div>

<div class="footdef"><sup><a id="fn.5" name="fn.5"
class="footnum" href="#fnr.5">5</a></sup> <p class="footpara">
<a
href="https://en.wikipedia.org/wiki/Big_data">https://en.wikipedia.or
g/wiki/Big_data</a>
</p></div>

<div class="footdef"><sup><a id="fn.6" name="fn.6"
class="footnum" href="#fnr.6">6</a></sup> <p class="footpara">
<a
href="https://en.wikipedia.org/wiki/Klondike_Gold_Rush">https://en.
wikipedia.org/wiki/Klondike_Gold_Rush</a>
</p></div>

<div class="footdef"><sup><a id="fn.7" name="fn.7"
class="footnum" href="#fnr.7">7</a></sup> <p class="footpara">
<a
href="https://en.wikipedia.org/wiki/El_Dorado">https://en.wikipedia.
org/wiki/El_Dorado</a>
</p></div>

<div class="footdef"><sup><a id="fn.8" name="fn.8"
class="footnum" href="#fnr.8">8</a></sup> <p class="footpara">
<a
href="https://www.economist.com/technology-quarterly/2018/06/02/i
ncreased-amounts-of-data-and-surveillance-are-transforming-justice-
systems">https://www.economist.com/technology-quarterly/

*2018/06/02/increased-amounts-of-data-and-surveillance-are-
transforming-justice-systems</a>*
</p></div>

*<div class="footdef"><sup><a id="fn.9" name="fn.9"
class="footnum" href="#fnr.9">9</a></sup> <p class="footpara">
<a
href="https://en.wikipedia.org/wiki/Arab_Spring">https://en.wikipedi
a.org/wiki/Arab_Spring</a>*
</p></div>

*<div class="footdef"><sup><a id="fn.10" name="fn.10"
class="footnum" href="#fnr.10">10</a></sup> <p
class="footpara">
<a
href="https://en.wikipedia.org/wiki/WikiLeaks">https://en.wikipedia.
org/wiki/WikiLeaks</a>*
</p></div>

*<div class="footdef"><sup><a id="fn.11" name="fn.11"
class="footnum" href="#fnr.11">11</a></sup> <p
class="footpara">
<a
href="https://en.wikipedia.org/wiki/Freedom_of_the_Press_Foundati
on">https://en.wikipedia.org/wiki/
Freedom_of_the_Press_Foundation</a>*
</p></div>

*<div class="footdef"><sup><a id="fn.12" name="fn.12"
class="footnum" href="#fnr.12">12</a></sup> <p
class="footpara">
<a
href="https://en.wikipedia.org/wiki/Whistleblower">https://en.wikipe
dia.org/wiki/Whistleblower</a>*
</p></div>

*<div class="footdef"><sup><a id="fn.13" name="fn.13"
class="footnum" href="#fnr.13">13</a></sup> <p
class="footpara">
<a
href="https://en.wikipedia.org/wiki/Edward_Snowden">https://en.wik
ipedia.org/wiki/Edward_Snowden</a>*
</p></div>

<div class="footdef"><sup><a id="fn.14" name="fn.14"
class="footnum" href="#fnr.14">14</a></sup> <p
class="footpara">
<a
href="https://en.wikipedia.org/wiki/General_Data_Protection_Regula
tion">https://en.wikipedia.org/wiki/
General_Data_Protection_Regulation</a>
</p></div>

<div class="footdef"><sup><a id="fn.15" name="fn.15"
class="footnum" href="#fnr.15">15</a></sup> <p
class="footpara">
<a href="https://www.britannica.com/biography/Richard-Matthew-
Stallman">https://www.britannica.com/biography/Richard-Matthew-
Stallman</a>
</p></div>

<div class="footdef"><sup><a id="fn.16" name="fn.16"
class="footnum" href="#fnr.16">16</a></sup> <p
class="footpara">
<a
href="https://en.wikipedia.org/wiki/Richard_Stallman">https://en.wik
ipedia.org/wiki/Richard_Stallman</a>
</p></div>

<div class="footdef"><sup><a id="fn.17" name="fn.17"
class="footnum" href="#fnr.17">17</a></sup> <p
class="footpara">
<a href="https://www.youtube.com/watch?
v=Gnw_K5DPkbc">https://www.youtube.com/watch?
v=Gnw_K5DPkbc</a>
</p></div>

<div class="footdef"><sup><a id="fn.18" name="fn.18"
class="footnum" href="#fnr.18">18</a></sup> <p
class="footpara">
<a
href="https://en.wikipedia.org/wiki/Massachusetts_Institute_of_Techn
ology">https://en.wikipedia.org/wiki/
Massachusetts_Institute_of_Technology</a>
</p></div>

<div class="footdef">^{<a id="fn.19" name="fn.19" class="footnum" href="#fnr.19">19</a>} <p class="footpara">
<a href="https://en.wikipedia.org/wiki/MIT_Computer_Science_and_Artificial_Intelligence_Laboratory">https://en.wikipedia.org/wiki/MIT_Computer_Science_and_Artificial_Intelligence_Laboratory</a>
</p></div>

<div class="footdef">^{<a id="fn.20" name="fn.20" class="footnum" href="#fnr.20">20</a>} <p class="footpara">
<a href="https://www.fsf.org/">https://www.fsf.org/</a>
</p></div>

<div class="footdef">^{<a id="fn.21" name="fn.21" class="footnum" href="#fnr.21">21</a>} <p class="footpara">
<a href="https://en.wikipedia.org/wiki/GNU">https://en.wikipedia.org/wiki/GNU</a>
</p></div>

<div class="footdef">^{<a id="fn.22" name="fn.22" class="footnum" href="#fnr.22">22</a>} <p class="footpara">
<a href="https://www.webopedia.com/TERM/K/kernel.html">https://www.webopedia.com/TERM/K/kernel.html</a>
</p></div>

<div class="footdef">^{<a id="fn.23" name="fn.23" class="footnum" href="#fnr.23">23</a>} <p class="footpara">
<a href="https://techterms.com/definition/kernel">https://techterms.com/definition/kernel</a>
</p></div>

<div class="footdef">^{<a id="fn.24" name="fn.24" class="footnum" href="#fnr.24">24</a>} <p class="footpara">

<a
href="https://en.wikipedia.org/wiki/Linus_Torvalds">https://en.wikip
edia.org/wiki/Linus_Torvalds</a>
</p></div>

<div class="footdef"><sup><a id="fn.25" name="fn.25"
class="footnum" href="#fnr.25">25</a></sup> <p
class="footpara">
<a
href="https://en.wikipedia.org/wiki/University_of_Helsinki">https://
en.wikipedia.org/wiki/University_of_Helsinki</a>
</p></div>

<div class="footdef"><sup><a id="fn.26" name="fn.26"
class="footnum" href="#fnr.26">26</a></sup> <p
class="footpara">
<a href="https://www.livescience.com/20718-computer-
history.html">https://www.livescience.com/20718-computer-
history.html</a>
</p></div>

<div class="footdef"><sup><a id="fn.27" name="fn.27"
class="footnum" href="#fnr.27">27</a></sup> <p
class="footpara">
<a
href="https://en.wikipedia.org/wiki/ARPANET">https://en.wikipedia.
org/wiki/ARPANET</a>
</p></div>

<div class="footdef"><sup><a id="fn.28" name="fn.28"
class="footnum" href="#fnr.28">28</a></sup> <p
class="footpara">
<a
href="https://en.wikipedia.org/wiki/Eric_S._Raymond">https://en.wik
ipedia.org/wiki/Eric_S._Raymond</a>
</p></div>

<div class="footdef"><sup><a id="fn.29" name="fn.29"
class="footnum" href="#fnr.29">29</a></sup> <p
class="footpara">
<a
href="http://www.catb.org/~esr/writings/cathedral-bazaar/cathedral-

bazaar/index.html">http://www.catb.org/~esr/writings/cathedral-
bazaar/cathedral-bazaar/index.html</a>
</p></div>

<div class="footdef"><sup><a id="fn.30" name="fn.30"
class="footnum" href="#fnr.30">30</a></sup> <p
class="footpara">
<a
href="https://en.wikipedia.org/wiki/Netscape">https://en.wikipedia.or
g/wiki/Netscape</a>
</p></div>

<div class="footdef"><sup><a id="fn.31" name="fn.31"
class="footnum" href="#fnr.31">31</a></sup> <p
class="footpara">
<a
href="https://www.economist.com/technology-quarterly/2018/06/02/i
ncreased-amounts-of-data-and-surveillance-are-transforming-justice-
systems">https://www.economist.com/technology-quarterly/
2018/06/02/increased-amounts-of-data-and-surveillance-are-
transforming-justice-systems</a>
</p></div>

<div class="footdef"><sup><a id="fn.32" name="fn.32"
class="footnum" href="#fnr.32">32</a></sup> <p
class="footpara">
<a href="http://www.pewinternet.org/2015/05/20/americans-
attitudes-about-privacy-security-and-surveillance/">http://
www.pewinternet.org/2015/05/20/americans-attitudes-about-privacy-
security-and-surveillance/</a>
</p></div>

</div>
</div></div>
<div id="postamble" class="status">
<p class="author">Author: Christer Foghagen</p>
<p class="date">First draft created: 2019-02-21 tor 15:51; Revised:
2021-01-13</p>
<p class="creator"><a
href="http://www.gnu.org/software/emacs/">Emacs</a> 25.2.2 (<a
href="http://orgmode.org">Org</a> mode 8.2.10)</p>

```html
<p class="validation"><a href="http://validator.w3.org/check?
uri=referer">Validate</a></p>
</div>
</body>
</html>
```

Your notes and comments

Reflections, thoughts and reactions goes here…

the ice is melting
thin light in a mist of joy
steel trains are coming